"Humble Beginnings"

An Expression of my Journey through Paintings and Poems

by
Timothy L. Giles

Editor: Sterling T. Giles
Illustrator: Timothy L. Giles

www.timgilesafroartsandcrafts.com
E-mail: timgilesafroartsandcrafts@yahoo.com

Acknowledgements

I want to first thank God for giving me the talent to paint! This is a gift that I will forever be grateful. It is a talent that I want to share with the world; whether helping young teens who have an ambition of becoming an artist or just showing and marketing my work.

My family and friends have been very supportive and I thank them all for their timeless efforts in assisting me with the completion of this book. Linda Bunch of the Suffolk Art League in Suffolk, Virginia has encouraged and supported me since I was a young man just learning my craft. My mother, Mary Alice Daniel had confidence in me and purchased me my first paint by number oil set, which started me on my way. I extend a special thanks to my editor, Sterling who is also my eldest teenage son. He desires to become a journalist and this was his first major project that put his career choice to the test. My wife, Lori was the technical expert in getting this book published. Her late nights working on this project was worth the wait. My youngest son Tyler was always there giving encouraging words and unconditional support.

To my readers, I hope you find solace in my paintings and poems when reflecting on some of the challenges of life, your search for inner peace or understanding the true value of family.

Contents

"Blessed are the Meek"

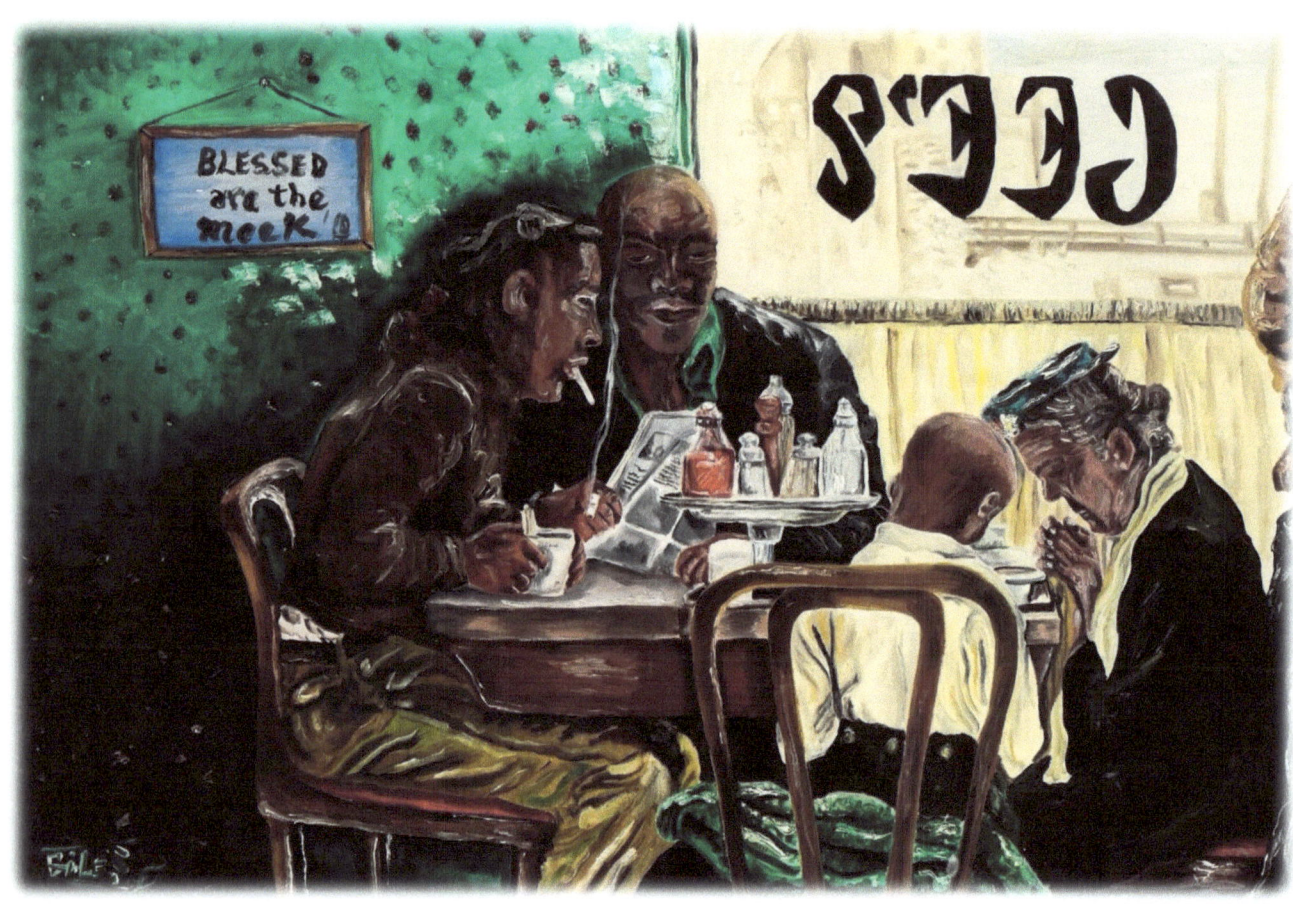

Blessed Are the Meek

Our father which art in heaven...I can't thank you enough,

There are two gentlemen at my table watching as I pray to you about all my "stuff".

My grandson and I can hardly afford the cost of this meal,

However, I am inclined to thank you Lord, still.

You have allowed me to walk with you since my young birth,

I know according to your words the meek shall inherit the earth.

Thank you for the opportunity to witness to these men who wonder as I pray, what it is that I seek,

I will simply say to them, "I love Jesus and he has a crown for the humble and the meek".

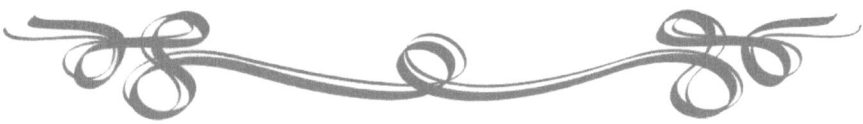

This particular painting was done in acrylic. It is one of my earlier pieces. I got the idea from a famous artist whose name I am proud to mention, Norman Rockwell! His work inspired me so much in my formative years and even today. All of his work has human emotion, character, activities, and situations. This is how I want my art to come across to the public. There is no denying that he is one of America's greatest artists. He allowed himself to be free and paint about common life experiences.

In this painting, the two burly men are watching the elderly lady and her grandson do something they are not accustomed to doing which is praying. The lady and her grandson probably don't have much in the way of resources, but they know they still must take time to give thanks to the Almighty.

Acrylics allow me to apply richer colors to my work. The drawback to using acrylics is that they dry much too fast for me to use often as a medium. I had fun doing the piece and as you can see, human conditions are the primary subject of my work.

"Buffalo Soldier"

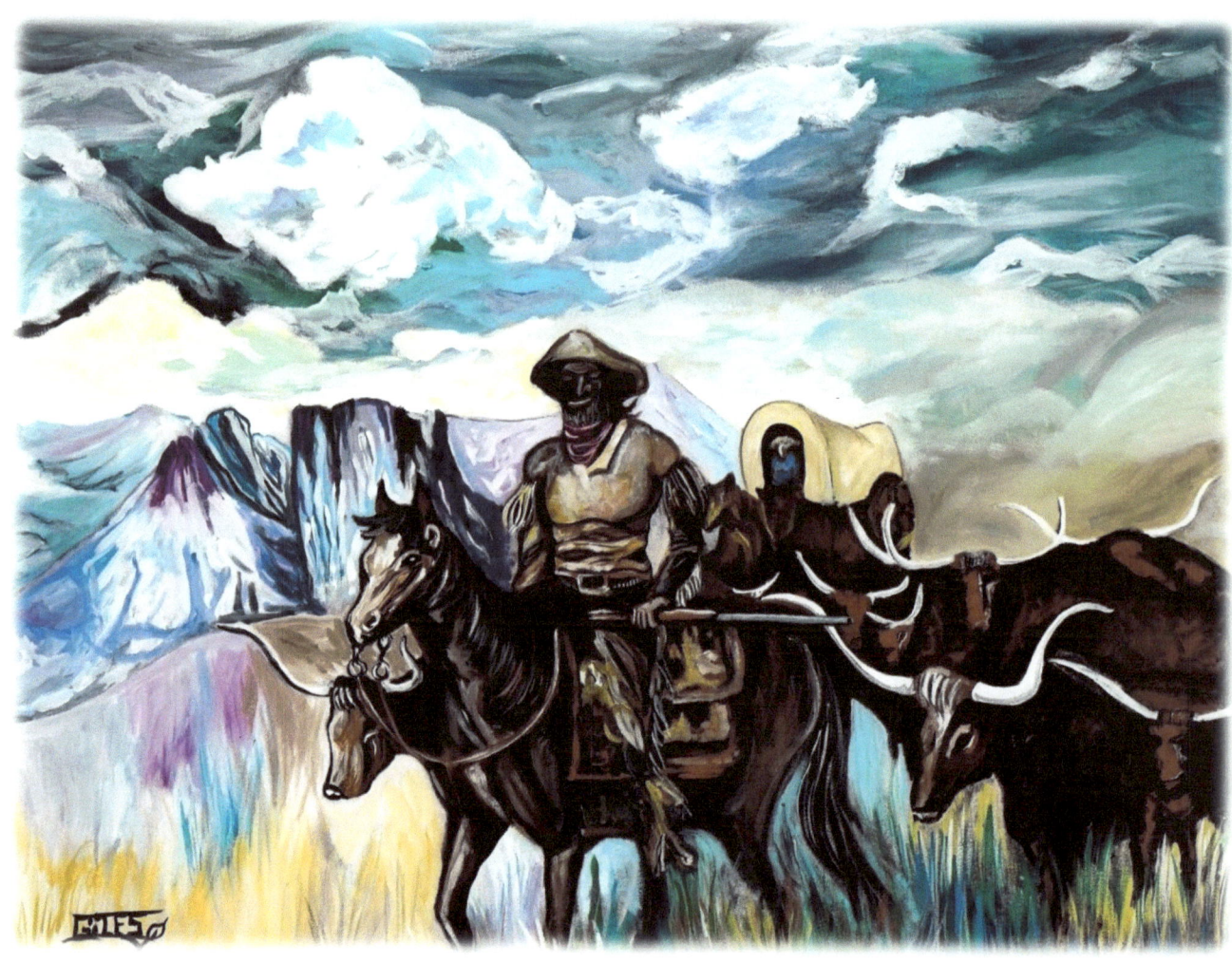

Buffalo Soldier

A fierce defender of the American West, life of this soldier, mobile and always on the go,

The Indians feared them and their blazing guns. When asked to describe them…"like a Buffalo".

Runaway slaves in some cases, just trying to find their piece of independence in this land,

Only a few generations; stolen from Africa brought to America; constitutionally, half a man.

Unparallel to all other fighters who roamed the vast western land and the Great Plains.

In spite of the unequal treatment by whites who ruled the government of yesterday,

These stern proud warriors whom never refused a challenge from their enemies are still unsung heroes today.

Whether a six gun shooter or a Winchester rifle in their hands ready to do battle,

These gentlemen represented the legacy of African-American's best as they drove hard in their saddles.

Eventually when their duties where done, they drove great wagon trains to explore the new West,

Other outfits applied for the dangerous job of guiding family and supplies through hills, plains and crests.

I am told by ole' timers that to see these men in uniform, lean, tall, and discipline was something to behold,

Many soldiers have fought for the red, white and blue, but none have come close to the Buffalo Soldier…the true, the proud and the bold.

Color, color, and more color! This painting was done in acrylics and I love the array of colors this medium offers. I love the old western type painting because the prairies and plains are alive with beautiful colors. I am a bit of a softy for history and will do extensive research before I paint such pieces, as I did with this one. I learned a lot about the pioneers of yesteryear and it set my mood for the painting. Each one of my paintings, just like a book, takes me places. I meet all sorts of interesting people. I am physically, mentally and spiritually committed to all the work of art that I do.

In this painting, I can literally imagine the dust being kicked up and the howling of the herd. The plain is wide open and the soldier is alert looking for snakes, or any other adverse thing that he may encounter while on the drive. Later in the evening, you can imagine the different colors seen on the horizon and the mountain tops.

I hope someone will be inspired by this painting and poem and research the exciting history of the Buffalo Soldier.

"Communion"

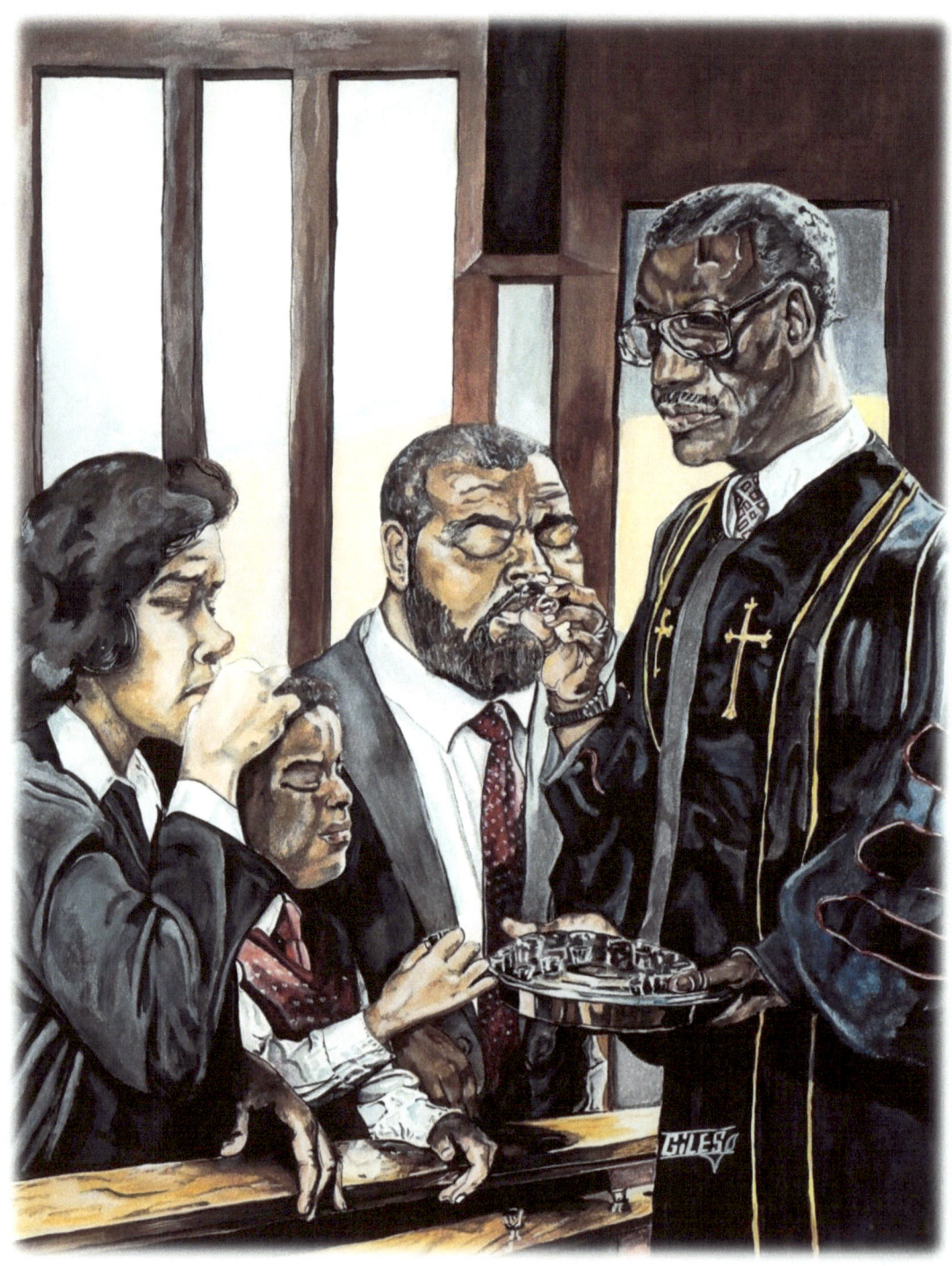

Communion

Take this bread in remembrance of me, your Lord and Savior,

Sip this cup of wine which represents my blood that I gave love and labor.

Jesus died at Calvary for us: man, woman and child,

To take communion if your soul is not correct with the Lord, would be defiled.

God so loved this world that He gave his only begotten son,

Jesus gave his life for humanity. You say you are one of his disciples, what exactly have you done?

He doesn't have the stomach for a lukewarm believer; a Christian with no bite,

However, he does need soldiers who are spiritually equipped for the fight.

Poverty, injustice and pure evil lurking in man's heart,

Giving thanks and praise is needed. So, when will you start?

You say your faith is like salt, which is a distinctive flavor,

Yet, your words without action mean nothing to the Savior.

Pick up your bread which represents His broken bone,

Now drink of His blood and prepare to commune.

I painted this picture in the early 1990s from a photo. I am a deeply religious person and this painting really moved me. The mother and father are taking communion with their young son. They both understand the representation of the bread and the wine being consumed. The bread represents the broken body of Jesus and the red wine is for his bloodshed. What fascinated me was the young boy's face as he tasted the wine. "Ugh!" seems to be his implied expression. He does not yet understand the importance of such a sacred ceremony.

The significance of this piece is that it is my first switch to painting with water colors. I really love the detail I am able to obtain when using this medium. I love the fact that if I make a mistake, I can easily erase and start over, with a little patience. I experimented with the wash method, which was taught to me in my high school art class.

"Daddy's Little Boy"

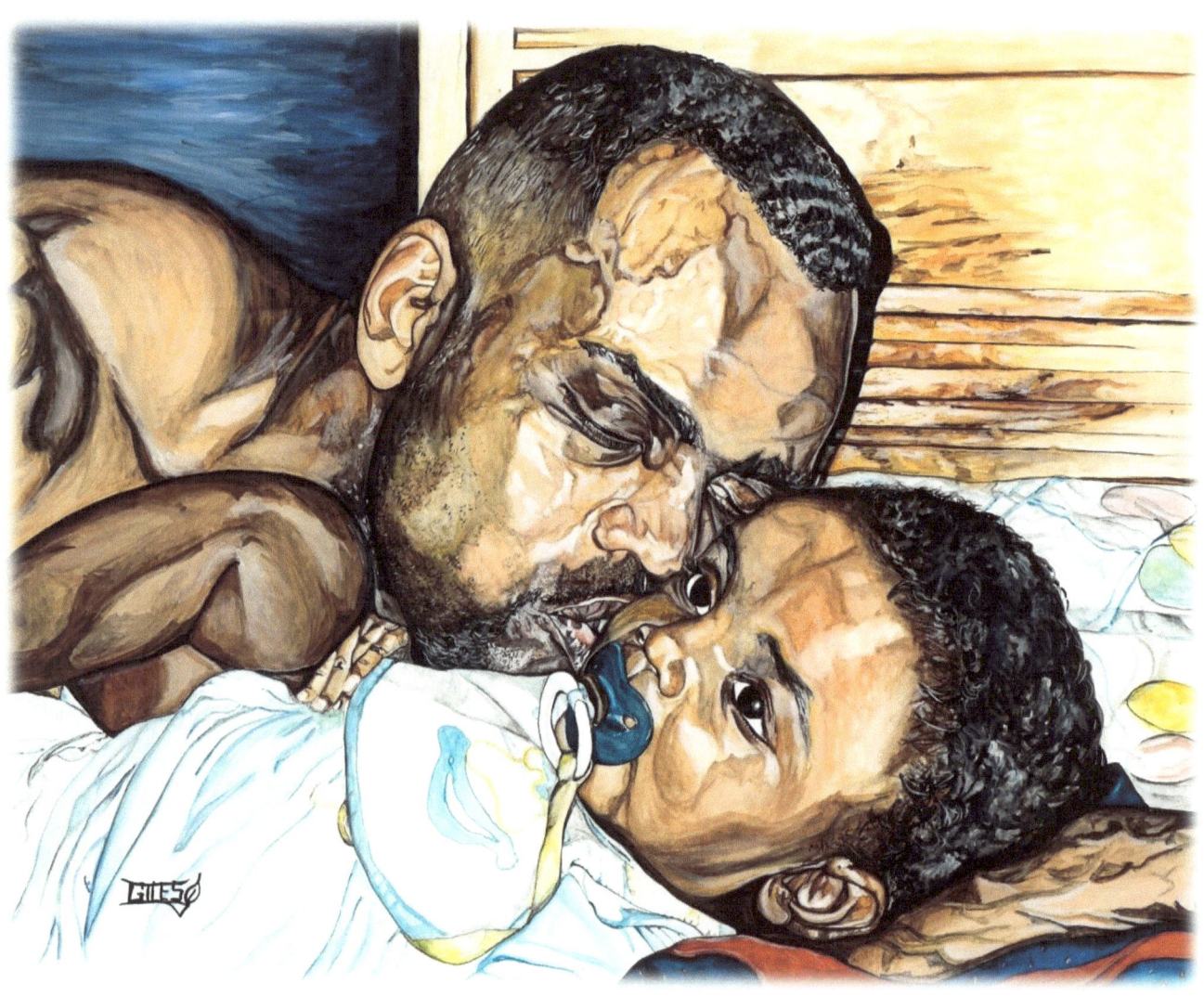

Daddy's Little Boy

He no longer looks at me with those needy little eyes, that comfortable stare; he knows I am here,

I watch him discover new things, stumbling through the house like a little soldier…no fear.

I remember when my day was hectic, but simply holding him calmed me so,

"Daddy… Daddy… look at me, no hands". I would reply, "Go my son…go!"

Such a masculine figure built like the Greek God, Hercules, strong and confident at thirteen,

A formidable student, intelligent, astute, brilliant, loving, all the qualities of a father's pride…pristine.

I often called his name, "Tyler!" You should have seen the smile that formed on his chubby little brown face,

My heart was full because I knew I had added another great African-American prince to the race.

What will he be, I thought…a doctor, lawyer, engineer, or maybe a great humanitarian working for all human beings.

Does he know that the Lord formed him in his mother's womb? Does he know he'll be a servant for the King?

It is six in the evening he hasn't called; I should not worry so much,

He's a good kid; not a bit of tainted blood running through his veins, but the streets, peers, and drugs, could become a crutch.

When he was small with curly hair, my little pride of joy, I could still hold him tightly in my arms,

I worried a lot less because I understood my responsibility as his father; protect him from all harm.

I can still remember him holding Batman, his favorite toy,

He's growing so quickly and he'll be gone soon. Slow down! Slow down!

How I miss my little boy…

I am an artist and know that composition hues, colors, etc. are important factors for a good piece of work. Those who follow my work know my inspiration is the subject matter. When I look at this piece containing my youngest son Tyler, who is now a teenager, brings me all kinds of warm memories. How could any man not enjoy fatherhood when he looks upon his seed's face? Look at his expression. He is in "la-la" land. I placed the kiss on his face due to my reflection on how fortunate I am to provide for such a wonderful gift from GOD. My wife Lori captured this photo because when they are a newborn, it's impossible to get enough hugs or kisses. He's absolutely counting on me to provide the things to sustain his life because as an infant, he's totally helpless.

For you new fathers, enjoy your children because they grow up quickly and the kisses are few and far between. As they get older, you may hear "Aw Dad, not in front of my friends".

He's growing into an incredible young man with good character, intelligence, looks and a very responsible teenager. I love my "little" boy!

"From Feast to Famine"

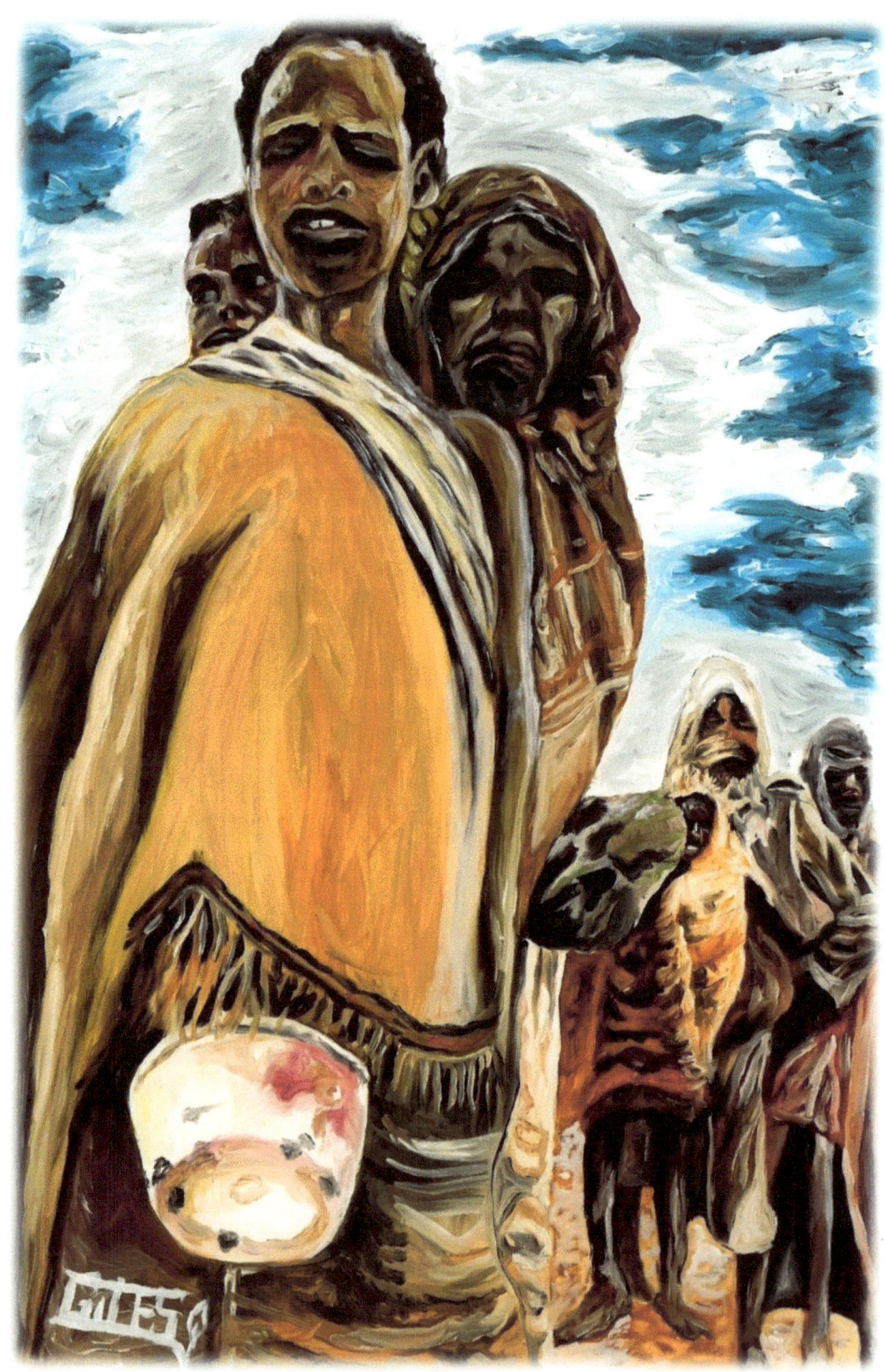

From Feast to Famine

Another year passes and Forbes Magazine writes stories about the richest people on earth,

During the 20th century an estimated 70 million died from starvation, many at birth.

Famines are caused by misguided economics, political design, war and GREED...a deadly sin,

While the world boasts of big houses, expensive clothes, jewelry, and their Mercedes-Benz.

We see commercials about massive starvation on a global level and we only say "poor folks",

This epidemic strikes Sub-Saharan Africa the hardest; hit with internal wars, babies and elderly dying. This is not a joke.

Governments brag about a hybrid strain of seeds; high yielding crops in the media they say,

Currently the continent can only feed 25% of its population; they have no money and just can't pay.

Actors in Hollywood just purchased a mansion in Beverly Hills for twenty million bucks,

Billionaires consolidated the world resources; manipulating governments. This really sucks.

Greedy African dictators boast of ruining their own countries under the cloak of nationalism,

Like Rwanda, millions of women, men and children die on the streets...what cynicism!

What happened to the simple days when having food, family and friends was more than enough,

When did the entire world forget about looking out for its fellow man in exchange for more stuff?

Francis is eight years old; forced to become a child soldier recruited from a village orphanage,

One nation under GOD we say; Christians we call ourselves, while coveting others wealth to seek patronage.

We place athletes, movie stars, money makers, dictators and corrupt businessmen in high esteem,

While people die where they stand due to widespread scarcity of water and food; they can only dream.

I am amazed how we can watch this horrid destruction in the world each day unfold,

While we continue to waste so many resources often in excess; my GOD our hearts have grown cold!

Can you believe some people actually think that the poor are purposely destroying their own environment?

Others believe this is a plague like in Moses' day when they said GOD did this and it was heaven sent.

Take a minute to reflect. Be honest and ask yourself, do I need all of the material things that I possess?

The majority of this world is slowly moving from feast towards famine. So, are you a part of the solution or the problem, which is a person who perpetuates this mess.

I think we should all work hard to achieve the great American dream and personal goals that we want to meet,

However, as a Christian my prayer is that the entire world can have good health, shelter, water and an abundance of food to eat.

I did this piece of work because I am deeply concerned with the state of the impoverished people of today. I find it hard to see women and children with their bellies swollen; living in poverty with a lack of food and water.

This is the second oil painting I've done in years. I used the dark color to represent the overcast nature of this entire situation. With all of the resources in the world, I can't see why we don't pool monies together to help these poor victims. I will use my GOD given talent to highlight social issues such as these and I will use many of the resources to help wherever I can with this situation. The world often boasts of not being able to purchase high end homes when these babies can't even get a cup of milk.

My art provides me the opportunity to speak to many different audiences whom I hope to enlighten to help out where they can with world hunger, both home and abroad. One of my closet friends said the painting is very morbid and makes them sad. His response brought about the impact I wanted which is awareness!

"Greeks"

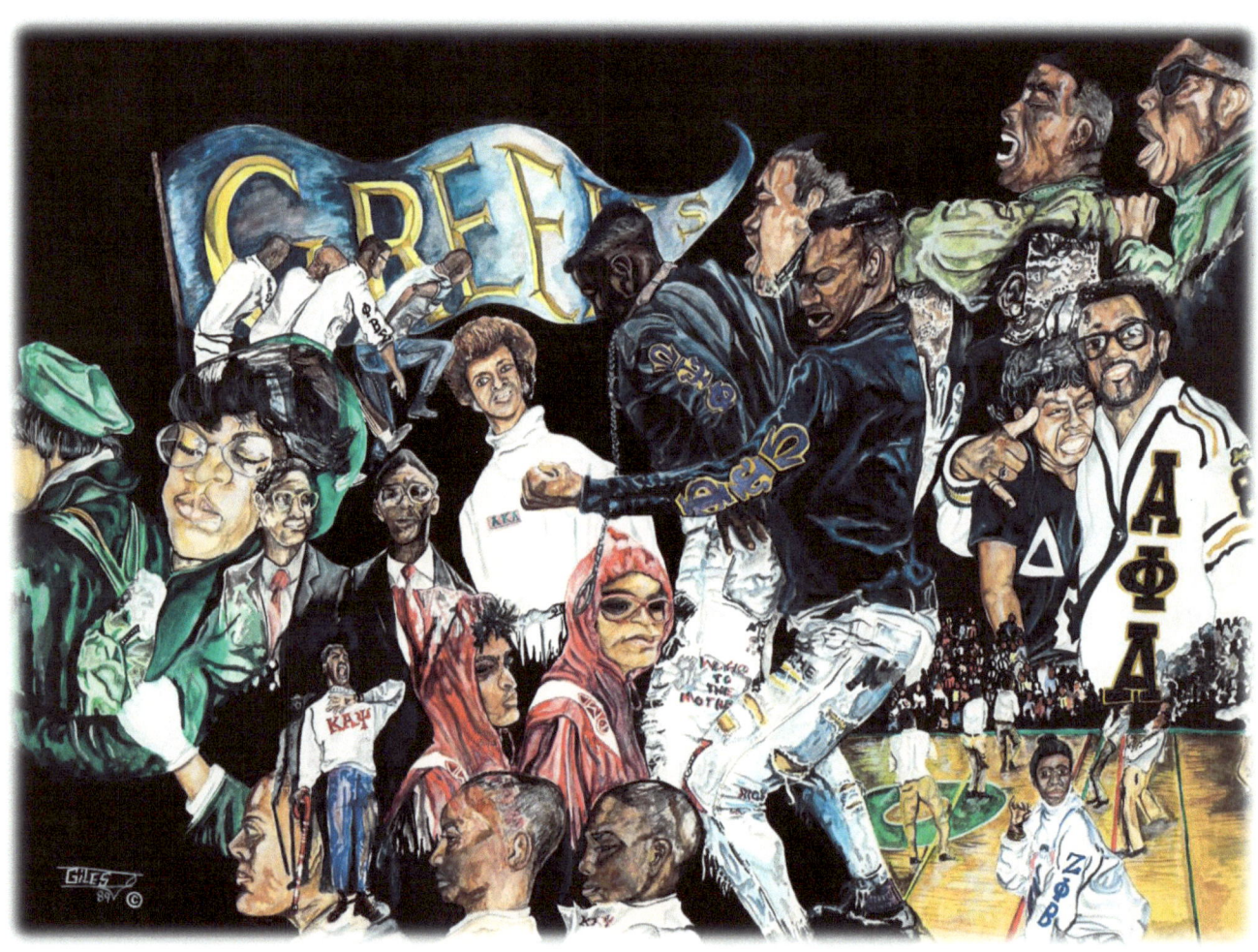

Greeks

Our commitment to excellence and leadership in our communities is our cutting edge,

The uplifting of African Americans as a whole is our goal when we pledge.

This organization recognizes that its goals are to mold young black women while providing an admirable shelter,

To cross over is no mere task; leadership, intelligence, loyalty and grace are only a few traits of a Delta.

Omegas are fearless; so you should grant them what they seek or prepare to brawl,

The purple and gold is a formidable foe of illiteracy, poverty, and injustice. Always on point are the Q-Dawgs!

At first glance, you would think these ladies are just another pretty face; but know they always have the plan of the day,

The pink and green are engaged with social challenges, one of the moral qualities of an AKA.

Alpha Phi Alpha, proud men of the black and gold; parallel to the theories of W.E. Dubois' Talented Tenth,

Educate my little brothers, the next generation to come. Providing them with a focus for the masses is what they meant.

Zeta, Zeta, always ready to put up a fight for what's right. Draped in their loyal colors of blue and white,

They understand if one is left behind it could spell disaster for the African-American plight.

Charismatic, good looking and dashing in their red and white; the professional Kappa is what they bring,

A frat with legendary members who are noted for social, political, and cultural change.

The mighty, mighty Sigmas in their blue and white,

Their constant commitment to our communities satisfies their plight.

A salute to the sororities and fraternities who have put forth the good fight for over a century or more,

Our prayer to God is that he continues to allow these organizations to produce leaders who are dedicated to the core.

Prideful and rightly so, fraternities and sororities give back so much to the African American community. Many of our most prominent leaders and business personalities are associated with one of these organizations depicted in this work of art. This painting in no way represents all of the Greeks that capture our culture on the campus of a HBCU, but a strong few. Many try to become members but not all possess the traits these great fraternities and sororities are seeking.

Familiar faces are seen in this painting as they are scenes from Hampton University, my wife's alma mater.

"The Horse Trainer"

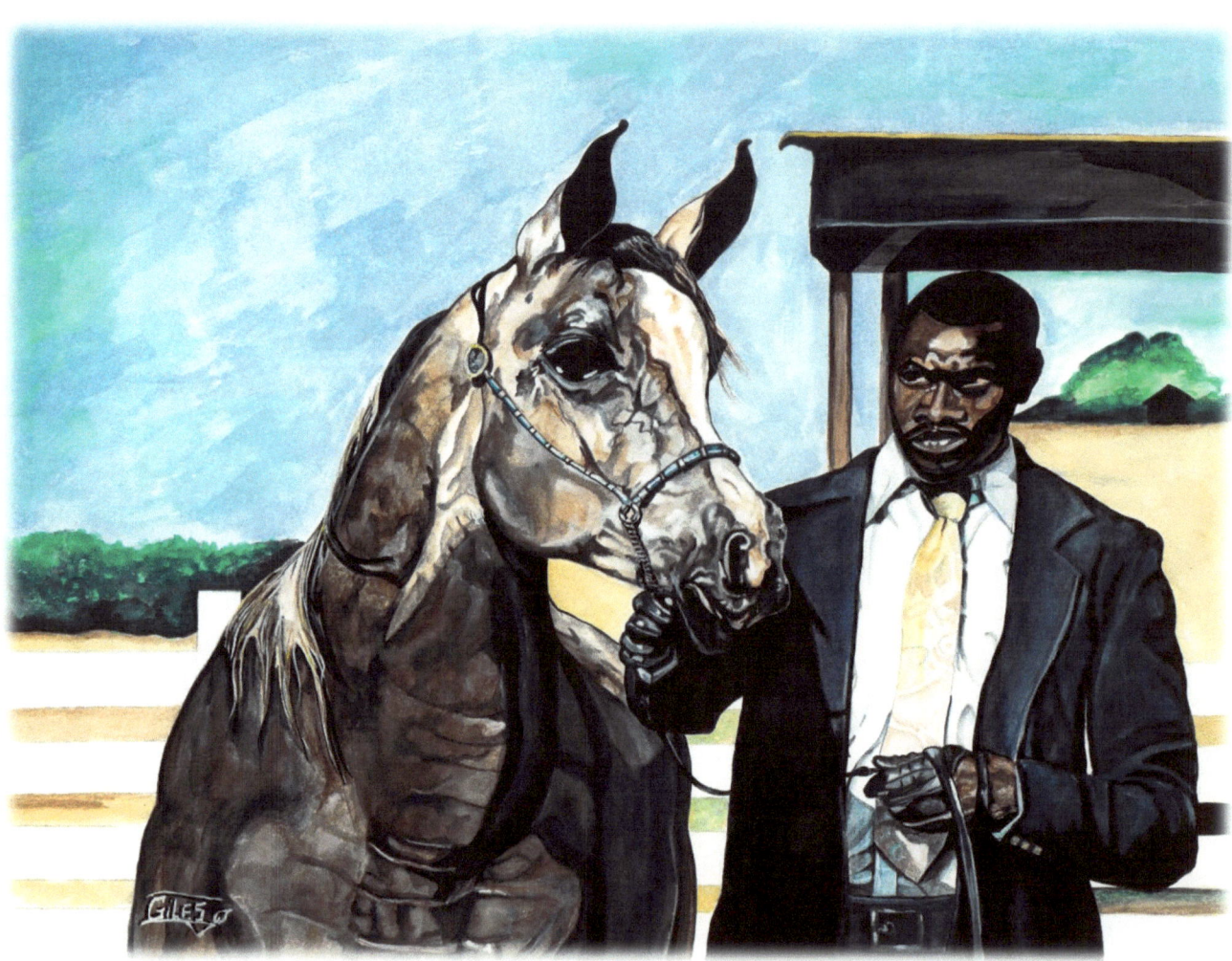

The Horse Trainer

I look deep into the strong beast's soul to see if I can control its spirit,

The horse looks back at me; another trainer who wants to ride, does he merit?

Not all animals are the same. Some stubborn and some are a little more accommodating,

Most newly broken horses are prideful and accustomed to being free; running and galloping.

We both dance the waltz because he doesn't know me nor I, him. The relationship is strained,

I tug on the reins and take a few laps around the track. I must let him know that I am "the man".

I am always amazed at such power and grace in motion; wild, yet waiting to be tamed.

I place the saddle on the horse's back. It moves continuously, not ready to submit.

I halt my efforts and take another walk. I feed him and converse for a while,

I look into its eyes again. I see a glimmer of hope. Was that a smile?

'King', a powerful stallion with the midday sun shining upon his silky black coat,

Finally he nods with approval. I mount the saddle, he gallops; I am afloat.

My efforts are rewarded. The bond is made and it's been a journey which almost drove me insane,

I am the master, you are my partner, and of the many horses I have broken you're the best I've trained.

I now understand your resistance; prideful stock captured and you were used to roaming free.

I give you my promise as a trainer to always treat you gently and with respect,

I am honored that you now accept me and there is no disconnect.

I painted this water color years ago when I still resided in Suffolk, Virginia. It's a painting captured from a photo of my cousin, Harold. We both attended John F. Kennedy High School until graduating in 1979. I had not seen him in years due to the different paths we chose in our careers. I attended a family reunion and was looking through Harold's photo album and came upon this photo. It captured both his and the horse's strength for me. It showed the strong character associated with my cousin. I found out that he had spent many years in Canada training thoroughbred horses. He explained to me that his time as a horse trainer was an incredible journey and capturing a piece of it on canvas was a treasure.

"Like Daddy, Like Son"

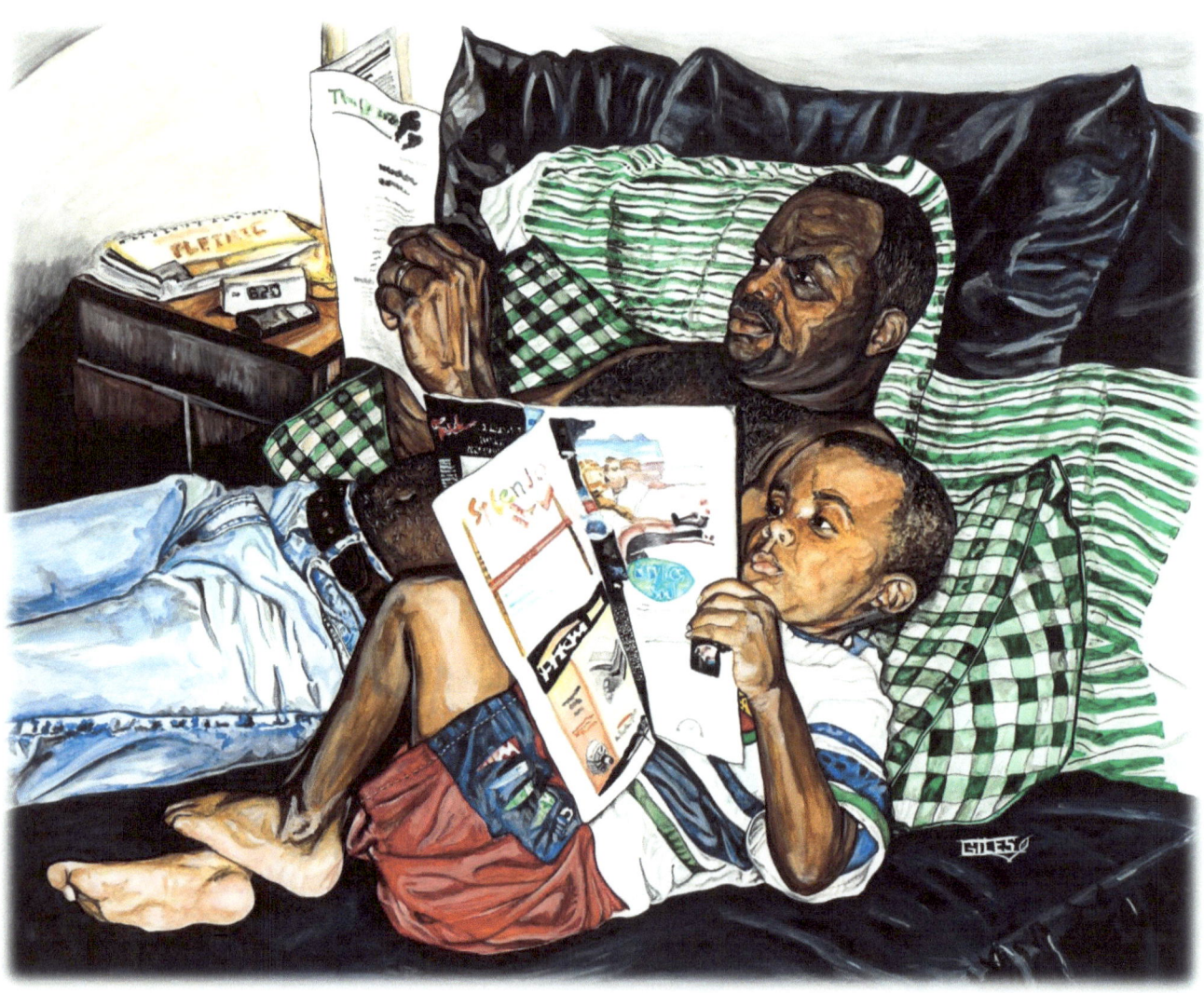

Like Daddy, Like Son

We have the power through grace and love to mentor a one of a kind,

An extension of ourselves; a branch of a tree that has endured the lessons of time.

I, the teacher, who has taught my student the rules of this life,

By watching me, hopefully he'll enjoy life's pleasures and avoid its strife.

Yes, I am a father, king and chief, an extension of my father and his father before,

I am the new legacy, an institution of knowledge to be passed on to the son whom I adore.

As my son smiles at me and looks over at my face,

He can be assured that I will prepare him for his legacy in this human race.

As a black man, I'll tell him he'll have to be twice as smart and that life isn't always fair,

But if he refers back to my lifetime of notes passed on to him, he'll surely make it there.

God first, family second, and then life on its own terms; focused he must remain and not ride both sides of the fence,

Serving the role of king, chief, and father, he will be responsible for passing on his knowledge to the next black prince!

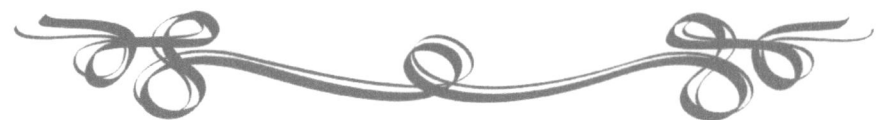

Instinctively, a son wants to mimic his greatest role model….his dad. Therefore, as black men we should accept the responsibility of serving as leaders for the next generation. Today, far too many of our youth are in prison, involved in gangs, on the streets, or deceased! Where is the father figure? Who's responsible for these young men? You could have the fortune of raising the next Martin Luther King, Jr., Malcolm X, Colin Powell, or President Barack Obama. There is also the possibility of just raising a productive, responsible, loving African American king who takes full responsibility in providing for his family.

The painting captures me and my eldest son, Sterling, relaxing on the bed catching up with the latest events. I found it amazing how this unrehearsed photo turned out. In fact, it was a surprise photo taken by my wife, Lori when we were living in Côte d'Ivoire, Abidjan as Diplomats. Sterling is turning into quite a leader. One of the top students in his class and he has a heart larger than life. He wants to become a journalist and will be off to college soon.

"Lil' Jazzy"

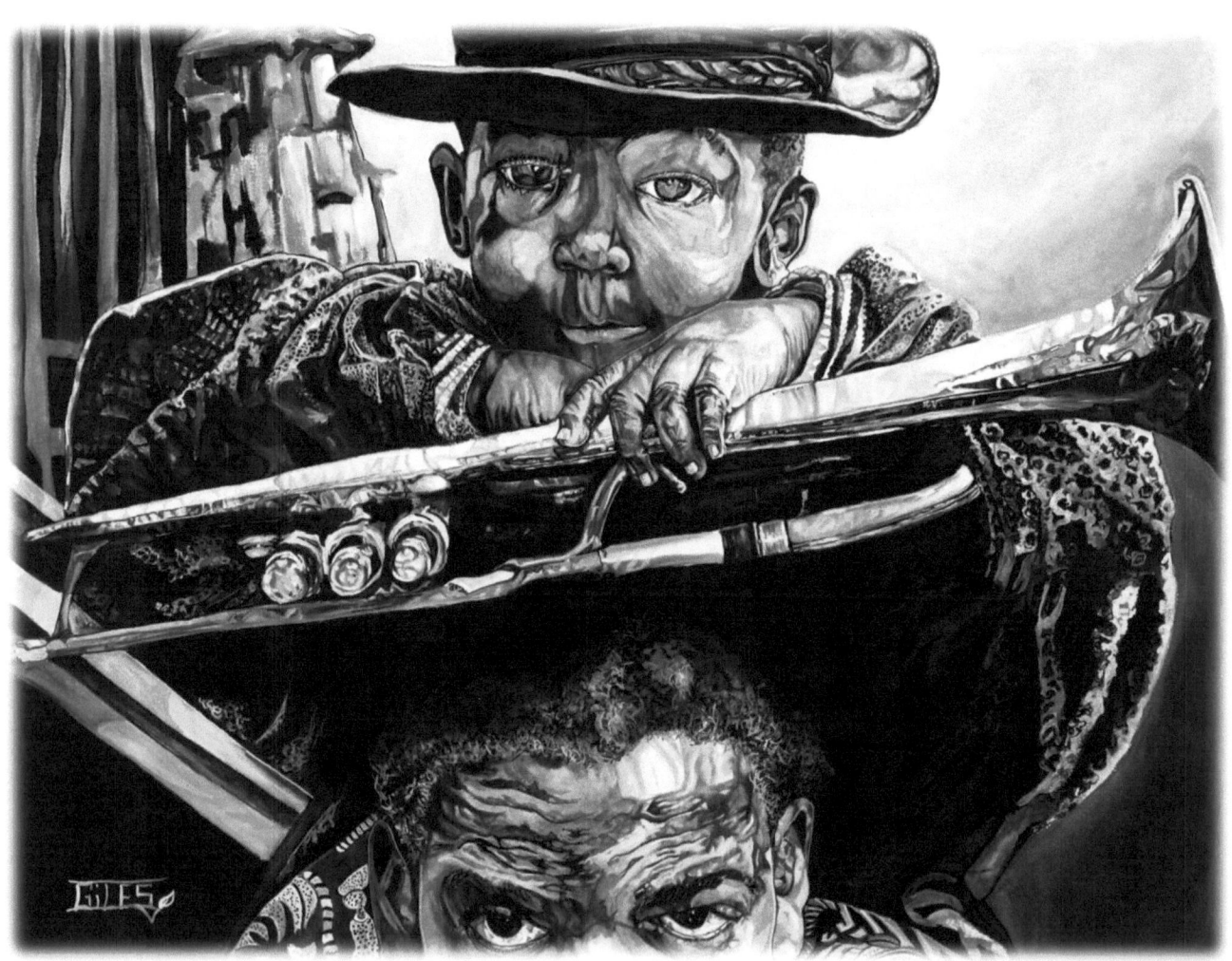

Lil' Jazzy

My Pops often spoke to me about the rhythm of a trumpeter.

He always becomes melancholy when he talks about all of the greats he's played with.

Gillespie, Miles...drinking their scotch, smoking their cigs and at curtain time confessing their souls through their tunes.

Bodies swaying...heads nodding in unison; each patron is treated by the legends' special gift.

I wonder how he does it; blast such a sweet sound from his trumpet with great ease.

Afro-Caribbean, classical, soul, and blues; a mental euphoria of music to one's ear.

The musician, my Pops, is playing as if he was seducing his audience; foreplay, a tease.

My heart beats to the rhythm of each note. They are ever so hypnotic calling me closer... "Come here!"

"Pop! Pop!" He can't hear me calling. He's playing like a mad man locked in a trance.

His dark glasses, black pin-striped suit...he's so cool. "That's my Dad", I tell the lady. "Isn't he classy?"

"Yes", she replied. "You're so cute. What's your name handsome?" "Lil' Jazzy!" "Blow Daddy! Blow!"

I am often touched when I see the display of love that fathers show for their sons. I absolutely think other than the bond between man and GOD, no two people can be closer from a man's perspective.

In this piece, I can imagine the father coming from practice at a local jazz club. His son comes back with him riding on his hero's shoulders as they walk down the block heading home. He can't wait to tell his mother about all the fun he had while visiting the club. I know Lil' Jazzy was very excited to see what keeps Papa away from home late nights during the week. I envision the proud dad taking his son around to meet his band members and telling them how one day his son may play for a large venue worldwide.

I assume my love of scenes like this between a father and son stems from the fact that my father left when I was about 7 years old. I recall the day vividly. He had his travel bag heading out the door for New York. We didn't spend any significant time together until I became older and went to work with him during the summer. I recall us having a very difficult time connecting. My message to fathers, spend quality time with your sons. Make them a priority and include them in your life.

This was the first water color in which I strictly painted with black and white. I absolutely love the contrast and plan to do more in this color scheme. This is one of my most favorite pieces.

"Midnight Blues"

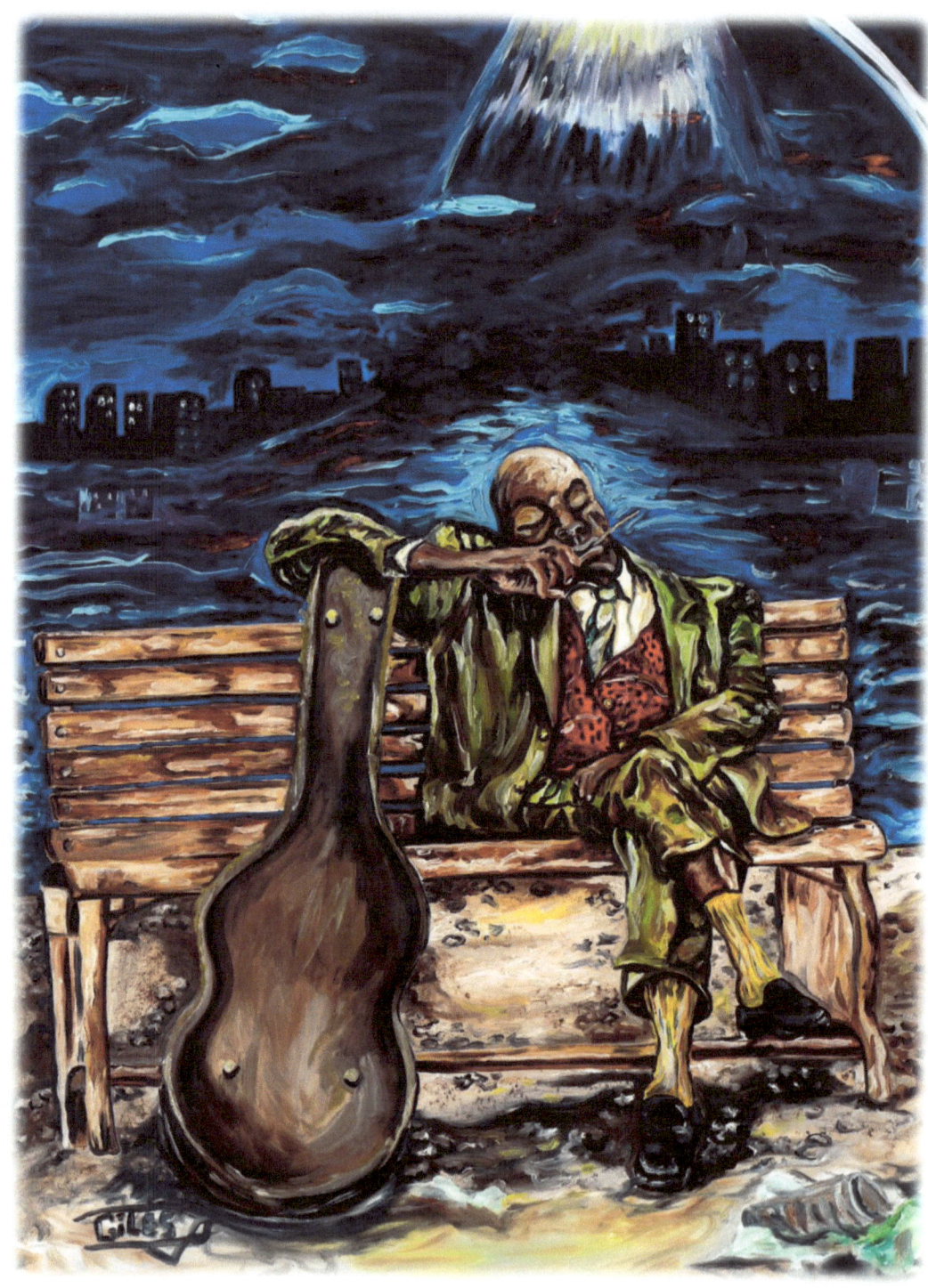

Midnight Blues

The crowd has gone home. The band is no longer playing its rhythms and melodies.

A beautiful lady passed me by as I left the club and she told me how much my music soothes.

The band members are seasoned musicians, who love the crowd and aim to please.

But tonight, my spirit is low and I am not at all amused,

The night air is still, my heart is heavy…I have the blues.

I think as I sit on this bench for a while contemplating on what I must do.

What happened to me? I used to enjoy this scene…booze, babes, and endless nights of fun,

We would come to the club, play a few sets, leave and party til' 5 a.m. The night had just begun!

So, when did I lose my ability to feel the beat and catch the sound?

Too much scotch perhaps? Drugs, meaningless risks to my family have brought me down.

I awoke this morning, hung over, listening to pillow talk…but I didn't enjoy the news.

Caught in another affair. It meant nothing, a groupie I thought.

After 22 years of marriage, she tried to stay but its over,

It's for real this time because I came home to an empty house. Now I feel the pain because I'm sober.

I'll sit on this bench 'til morning thinking of how I missed all of the clues,

But, its already midnight and I'm still feeling the blues.

I love music! I am addicted to the sweet sounds of instruments being played in harmony together. I created this painting from thoughts and visuals in my head. My influence was Ernie Barnes, a well known African-American artist. His style captivates me.

My vision of this subject matter is what I believe a musician would do when he just wants to clear his mind and reflect. Oil was the medium used for this painting. I love painting with oils because it allows me to move more freely with my brush strokes. I can merge the colors extremely well without the fear of crossing boundaries. I look at the captivating sky lines of the city and I can feel him enjoying the cool summer breeze coming off of the water.

I have gotten numerous compliments about this piece; it is one of my top sellers. I haven't done many paintings in oil; however, I will indeed do more work in this medium in the near future.

"The Fisherman"

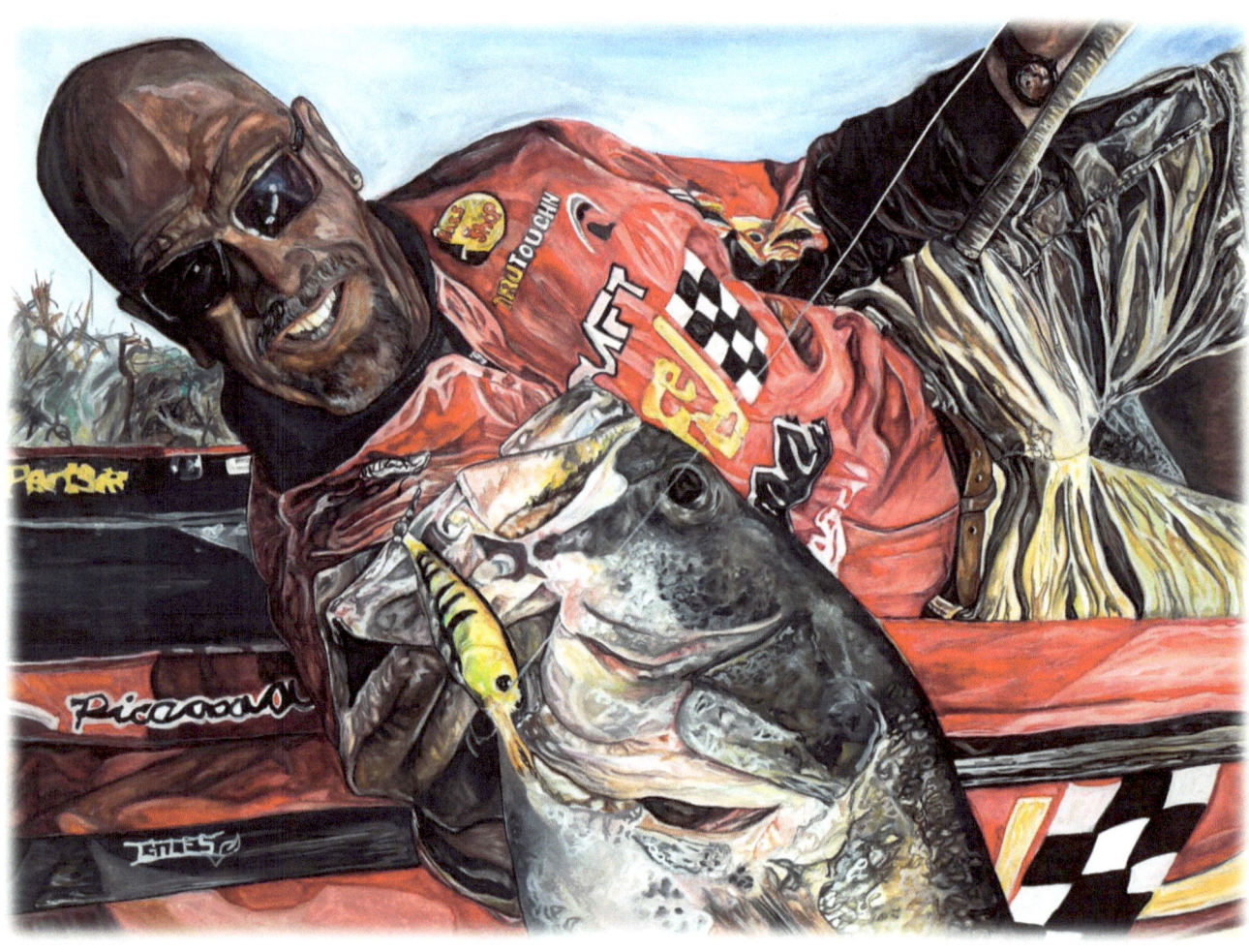

The Fisherman

I am sitting on the banks of the Chesapeake...a country boy, doing what I enjoy,

The music of the tide rolling in and out as my boat sits immediately off of the shore.

My hook is a perfect camouflage dressed with colorful lures and sometimes bait,

Whether salmon, tuna, pike, yellow perch, I just love fishing and cannot wait!

It's now noon and my cooler is looking pretty bare. A snag, I thug, and reel it in; under 2 pounds,

I have been here all morning; I am looking for the "Big One", so I think I'll hang around.

Fishing is not a sport where the average person is really concerned with time,

In fact, it's the perfect activity when you just want to sit and clear your thought filled mind.

Look at the boys faces as they reel in their first ever prospect from the water,

I am proud that my father also took me fishing; even today I still tell this story.

We are returning home with a loaded cooler full of fish. My sons are elated. "Hooray"!

My wife says, "Move them outside, they smell and whose going to clean those things anyway?"

My helpmate, I need her as I try to smooth things over,

"Did I mention I will make the macaroni and cheese, cornbread, and greens", as I look humbly over my shoulder.

I have not picked up a fishing rod in years. I saw this picture in a magazine and said this guy looks like he's in heaven. I love the colors and immediately thought this would make a great painting. Capturing my attention was the big mouth bass and the colors. Capturing this detail on canvas I knew would be a challenge. I proved myself correct; it absolutely was a challenge.

For those artists who have a love for painting animals in their natural environment, it's no cake walk in the park. This is due to the many details involved in portraying a real scene on canvas. However, once accomplished, you simply sit back in awe at the vividness of the work.

"Sisters on One Accord"

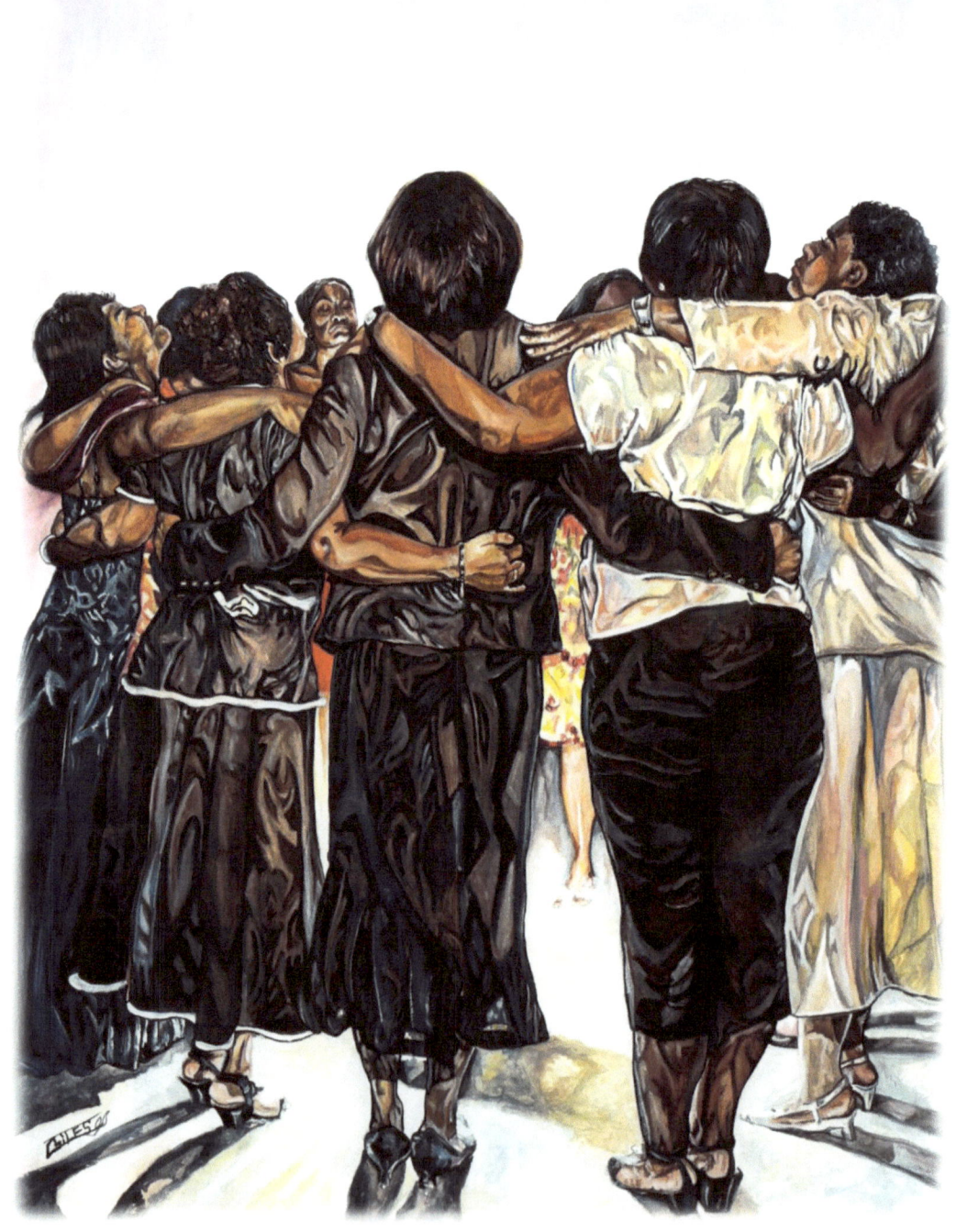

Sisters on One Accord

The troubles of this world we just can't avoid,

Sinful secular wants often cause us to take wrong detours.

It is so easy to allow ourselves to become disobedient due to the flesh, which craves satanic usage.

The enemy roams to and fro until we are finally destroyed,

We can prevent his attacks by putting our faith in the Lord.

There is something about a mother, a sister, an aunt, and a grandma together in a harmonious circle sending up "Godly" praise; knowing that Jesus is still in charge of those hard and trying days.

So, don't give up and become annoyed, unfocused, disobedient, and a back-slider by not serving the Lord,

You should always seek prayer...advice from sisters who are all on one accord.

    I am a Christian, so doing this water color of women embracing, and praising God was easy for me. I tend to paint with a lot of detail which is my trademark, but I don't want to lose the humanism of my work during the technical aspect of producing a new piece. I captured the detail in the dresses, shoes, the colors, etc.

    I seek emotion. I want you to feel this and join in the circle and also send up your requests. Live in the moment of these women who are in conversation with God on one accord. My motivation was the expressions on their faces. Take a moment and look at this picture. Close your eyes...makes you want to say, "Thank you Lord!"

"The Elder"

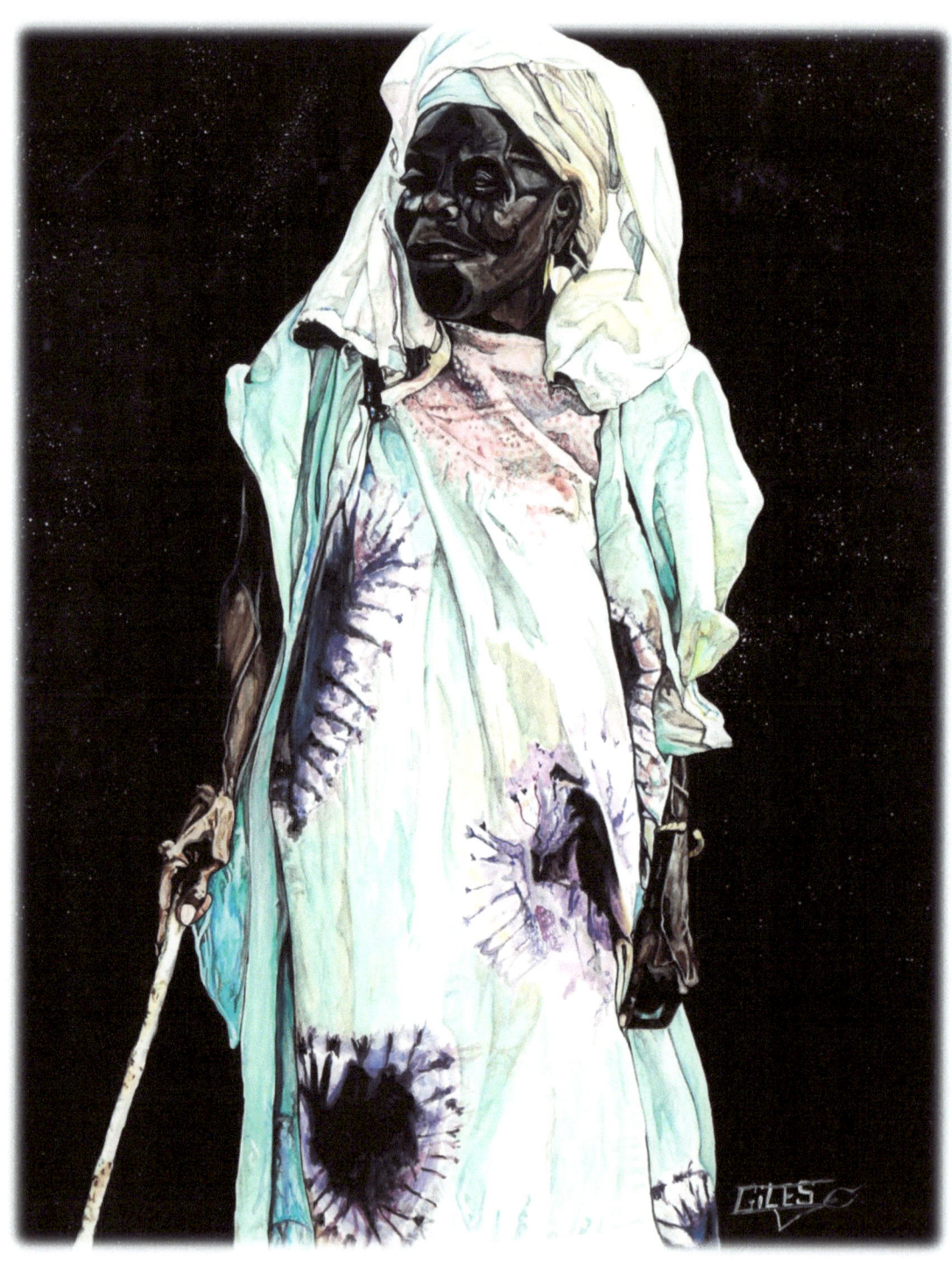

The Elder

I agree there are times in life when one wants to just give up,

Your family is torn apart, your man is not acting right, and you just lost your job.

The corridor of your soul is silent, empty, desolate...there is no sound,

The elder listens alternatively; forged through years of knowledge, experience, and wisdom by the pound.

"Quiet my love. Have a seat by me right here on the ground,

My eyes can't see as well as they used to.

My ears don't take in as much as they used to, but they do discern what is good for my life.

My hands are frail without the strength of yesterday,

But, I'm holding onto HIS word anyway!

I use my walking stick to steady my body because I have grown old,

I lean on the words of Jesus to brace my humble soul.

One century old; you can see my past troubles by the lines on my face,

But the way to becoming an elder is through God's loving grace.

So, surrender those problems to Him---your job, your family and your man,

It's impossible for you to change your problems with only human hands.

I learned as an elder that life is not always for the swift or just,

Your life will be fruitful by thanking God for His mercy and grace. It's a necessity and a must!"

When I started this picture, I was first taken by the colors of the villagers' exotic dresses. The reason for such dress was because of a ceremony to celebrate the "Queen Mother" of a particular village in Abidjan, Côte d'Ivoire, West Africa.

However, once I dove into the painting I was redirected due to the look on the elderly woman's face. Her expression speaks volumes. It told me that she had lived for approximately 100 years; it was also apparent that she had survived all that life had sent her way. Now, she was available to mentor the next generation about the troubles of life.

The "Queen Mother", is probably second in command as a village advisor (below the chief of the village). As I embarked this picture, the paint seemed to flow from my hands as I allowed her to enter my spirit. I executed on paper what I thought might be her frame of mind as she was recognized by her fellow villagers for achieving the milestones in her life.

Technically, it was a very challenging piece because of the skin tones and the texture of the garment. I originally had 5 other subjects in this picture but it took the focus away from the subject piece, the "Queen Mother".

I am absolutely motivated by tradition, especially when it serves the betterment of the many instead of the few. Truly, the world is just a small village and there is no substitute for wisdom than from our elders!

"The Promise"

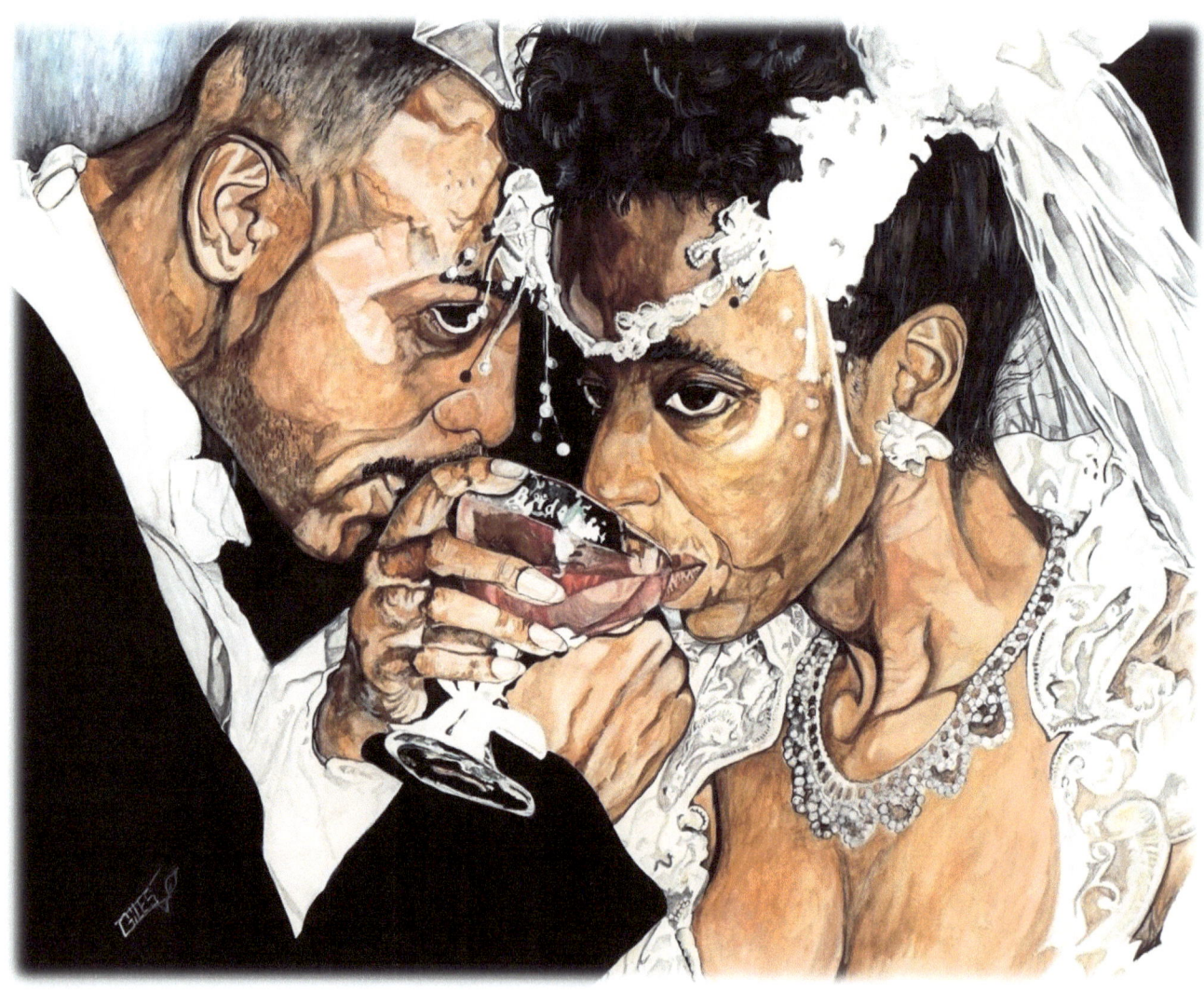

The Promise

"Dearly beloved, we are gathered together in the sight of GOD",

So many years of life's ups and downs; children, bills...man, its hard!

"To join this man and this woman in holy matrimony",

I grew, she grew...not together but, apart. Now we are talking divorce and alimony.

"Not to be entered into lightly but reverently, discreetly, solemnly."

She did her dirt and I typically chased skirts. Now, we want to be free.

"If any person can show just cause why this man and this woman may not be joined together, let them speak now or forever hold their peace".

If I had the wisdom then that I have now; emotion, notions, struggles...let this madness cease!

Marriage is the union of a husband and a wife in heart, body and mind,

Then how can two people start on a journey of commitment and love but it changes over time?

We make commitments together to face our disappointments, embrace dreams, realize our hopes,

We broke commitments, blamed each other for our disappointments, forgot dreams... vows broke.

Aspire to these ideals throughout our lives together – mutual understanding – openness,

We're both tired now because we have changed. At a cross road, headed in separate directions...we need rest.

"We are here today – before GOD – because marriage is one of HIS most scared wishes",

Yes, we love each other. The storms have been many but there is still love. LORD, I promised, but I don't know if I can survive life pulls and pushes.

"And now through me, GOD joins you together in one of the holiest of bonds",

I think back on life when it was carefree. I can remember when life was fun.

"And so, by the power vested in me and Almighty GOD, I now pronounce you husband and wife",

We planned…Life happened…We changed…What do we do for the remainder of our life?

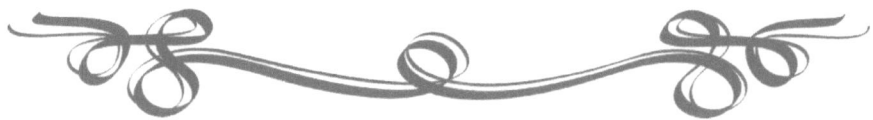

First, the disclaimer: This poem is not about my wife and I, but rather about the challenges couples sometimes face and try to work through in order to hang onto their marriage.

Ironically, the painting is of me and my wife on our wedding day. Because it was such a momentous occasion, one would immediately assume my poem would focus on the commitment and rosy experiences of a marriage. However, I thought I would try another approach. My wife and I have been together for over 22 years and it's mostly been bliss, but we've had our challenges. The point of this piece is that although challenges will come, couples should remain together and work out their issues. Young married folk today are too quick to divorce. Marriage is about the commitment of two people staying together for better or worse, in sickness and in health, until death do they part! These are not just words that are confessed during a ceremony but reality when the ceremony is over.

I recall when my wife and I were having some trying issues and I placed a phone call to my eight-five year old grandfather, Warren G. Williams. I spoke to him about our problems. He listened. After I spoke, he calmly said, "You married her, right?" "Yes", I replied. "And you did say for better or for worse, right"? Not exactly what I wanted to hear, but what he said was correct. "Timothy", he said, "being in a marriage is not just about you—don't you understand this? A selfish man will continue to say 'I, I, I', but mature men of GOD who understand the commitment that he vowed will always consider the 'us' in a marriage". These were wise words from a wise man.

As the years grow, we understand our love and God's favor will take us through our challenges in life.

"Three Moses', One Promise"

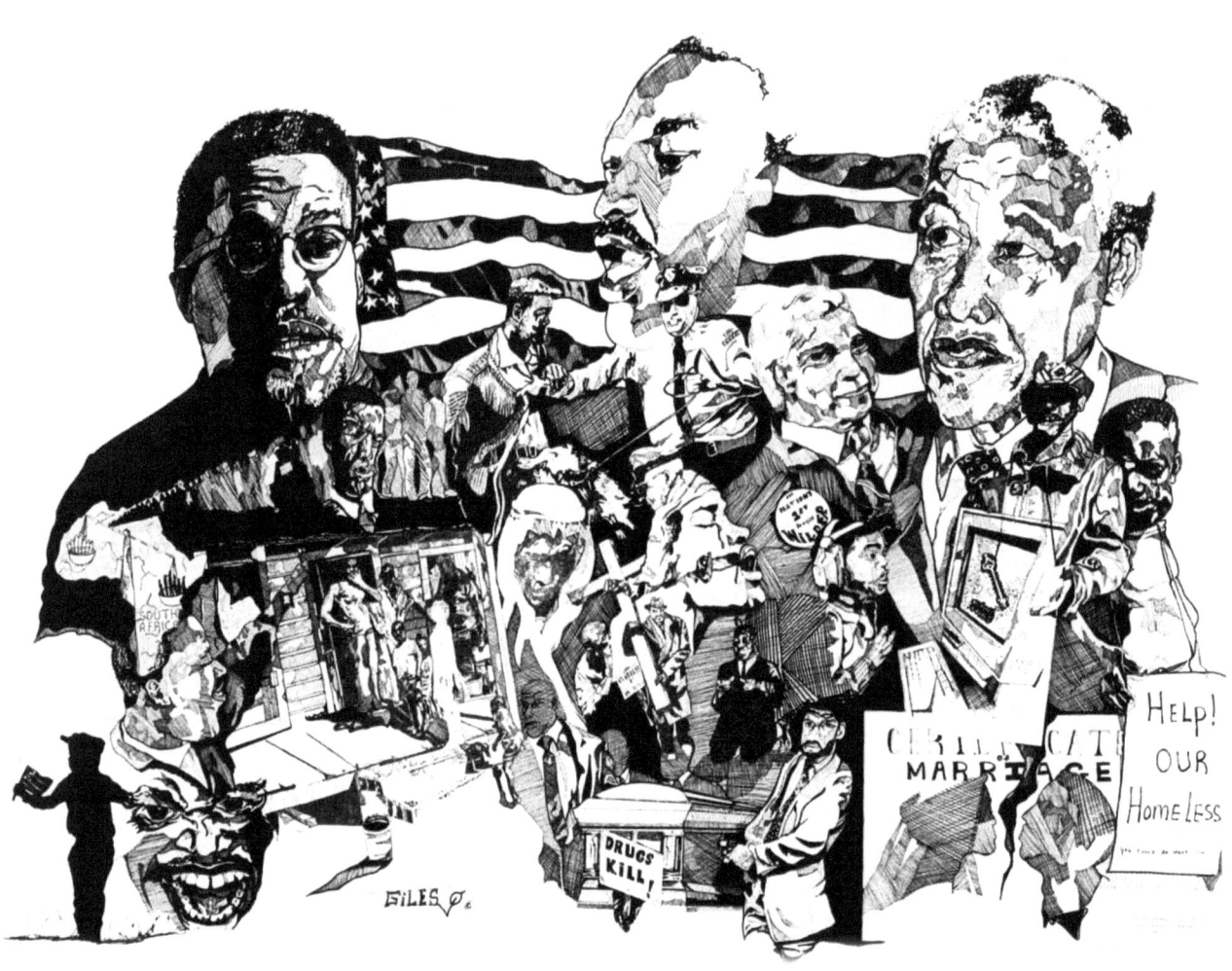

Three Moses', One Promise

As a brotha' from the 60's, I am asking what happened to the flow,

Malcolm, Martin, and Mandela asked Pharaoh to let their people go.

Like the Israelites, our people are walking in a circle today, lost in the desert sands.

Six decades of struggle to have a generation lost to jail, drugs and thugs.
Please let my people go!

Three hundred million precious African lives lost while crossing the seas,

Hundreds of negroes lost; hung on the branches of southern trees.

Let my people go!

Malcolm said, "A revolution by any means necessary!"

Martin said, "Emancipation through non-violence."

Mandela proved that destiny is inevitable by becoming head of state,

Yet, through all their struggle, bloodshed, and sacrifice, a great deal of our black men we cannot educate.

Let my people go!

Our families are deteriorating at an alarming rate,

Men no longer find it favorable to put food on their family's plate.

"No sense of pride," our women often say,

Another brother went to jail, another died today.

Let my people go!

Many strong black leaders died building our country---this red, white and blue,

Black civilization has suffered, people killed for me and you.

Brother, why not educate, embrace family, have structure, love, and prayer in your life?

Please let my people go!

If it takes a village to raise this generation,

Why don't many participate?

If it takes a village, why murder, jail, divorce, be self-centered, and inflict self-hate,

Why have many of our youth chosen this as their ultimate fate?

Let my people go!

Brothas' and sistas', how long will we continue on this destructive journey wasting our own time?

When will we start using the ultimate weapon...our own creative minds?

The kings and queens from Africa forced to build this red, white, and blue,

I am a black man responsible for my village, my wife, my sons and family too.

Moses asked, "Can you please, just let my people go?"

Go...go where? Will you lead them?

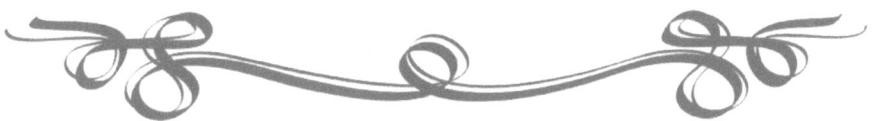

This pen and ink drawing speaks volumes to me and I hope to the viewer. It really tells a lot of stories if you look past the lines on the paper and look deep into the subject matter of the drawing. It speaks to the ills of the African-American and our struggle with life's challenges. Those challenges could be poverty, senseless deaths from drugs, violence, alcohol, or even society as a whole on an international scale.

Africans and African-Americans are joined by culture that will never be separated no matter the distance, time, location, or social condition. Although we reside in different hemispheres, our legacy intersects by our history. In fact, the drawing depicts the exodus from Africa to America. It illustrates that racism and bigotry has no real borders. Finally, the drawing shows that through each struggle, strong confident African American leaders have risen to advocate for our causes...freedom, justice, a right to pursue happiness and equality for all. Although their leadership style differed, ultimately they sought to change the unfair treatment of black men and women, simply due to their creed and color.

We believe in the banner of the American constitution and its preamble. Even abroad, America is a beacon for other nations seemingly lost and struggling with the poor treatment of a sector of the country's population. One of the three men in this drawing, Nelson Mandela, fought for equality in South Africa and spent numerous years in prison defending his belief in equality. Eventually, God's message of "love one another" resonated in his country and through real leadership; he chose not to be bitter by the consequences of his struggle for freedom. He led his country in a new direction of tolerance, respect, and freedom.

Our own, Dr. Martin Luther King, Jr. and Malcolm X, forged new movements of freedom and equality in America. Martin's rule was victory through non-violence because "hate for hate" resolves nothing. Malcolm X believed we should pursue our human rights as African-Americans "by any means necessary".

In conclusion, they all expressed the same need as Moses when he met with the Egyptian leader of the old days..."Let Our People Go"!

"Village Mother"

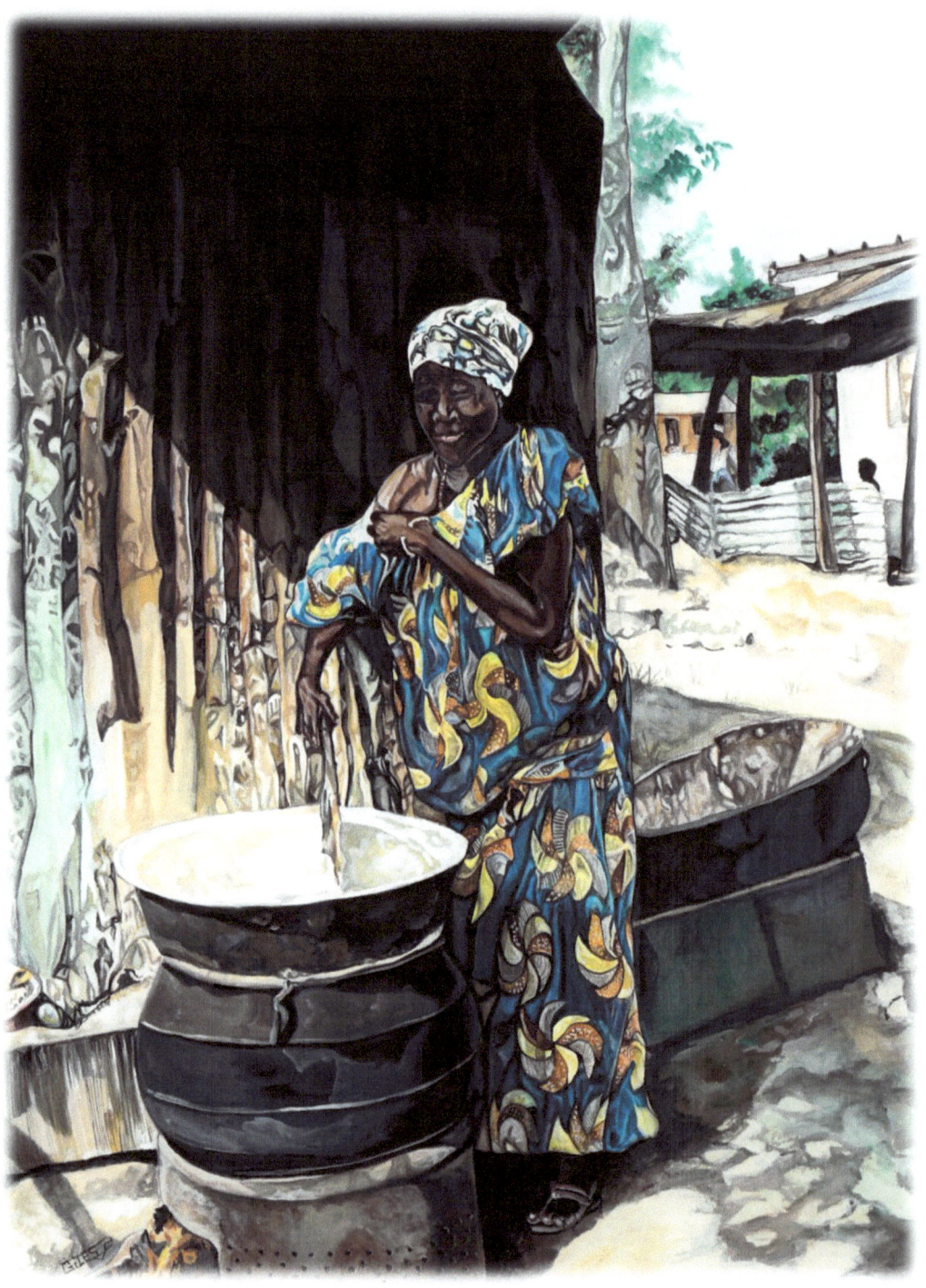

Village Mother

She understands more than any other her role to provide nourishment for the village.

Her unconditional love, preparation and commitment to feed the families of her clan.

Her morning begins early. A walk, a long walk to fetch water for others.

She stumbles from the weight of the load.

Her strength is reinforced by other mothers passing on the road.

She later pounds cassava, the meal of the day. Thump! Thump! Thump! Her arms grow weary from the laborious work,

The husband, kids, and others are just starting to move around, not yet alert.

"Where are my spices, spoons, pots, and pans?"

As she gathers the utensils, she knows by this open fire stirring for hours she will have to stand.

It's early, but the African sun rose many hours ago and the day will surely be hot.

"Kwame, Grace, Theo, come let me check you before the morning meal then off to school".

A grumpy husband finally awakes from his slumber and asks, "Can we eat? Where is the food?"

A slight glance in his direction and a lovely smile assures him that it will be ready soon.

It's done! Another morning meal prepared by the hands of a loving mother.

She grabs a bundle of branches and sweeps the loose dirt from the hut floor and the surrounding grounds.

Not often spoken but understood, the survival of this village is due to the unconditional love of the village mother.

Now that everyone is nourished and on their way, Kwame, the youngest, looks back and says,

"Mother, I love you!" She smiles...she understands.

I lived three years as a Diplomat in Ghana West Africa. While there, a friend gave me a photo which showed his mother preparing breakfast for several family members in his village in Accra, Ghana. I captured this lovely woman in water colors.

The lively colors in the attire are unmistakable no matter where you venture in the world. Just having the opportunity to set foot on the motherland was truly enough of an experience for me. This cultural exchange will never be forgotten. I have spent several nights in the village and had the opportunity to see firsthand the timeless preparation the women of the village put into each meal; no fast foods in these humble surroundings.

I saw what teamwork really means when preparing a meal in the village. Someone would have to literally walk to the local water source, which could be miles away, and fetch water. One pounding cassava, yams, another taking care of the vegetables, and someone else getting the pots, fire and other utensils prepared. What's so incredible is that this process is done daily for each meal for all of the families. The setting consists of old tin houses, "clean" dirt floors, bowls made from a calabash, big black pots and food cooked over an open fire. This may not be an ideal experience for the American woman because the men of the village usually sit around and discuss topics or business of the day while the women toil away with their duties. I was amazed even after the work needed to prepare the meals, the women still had energy to get the kids ready for school and many would spend a great deal of their day selling products on the roadside. The selling of products is a necessity in order to provide food for their families.

Family time is indeed family time in the village; no distractions such as televisions or radios which are so common in the American household. Sitting and having conversations about their day is their entertainment. I assume this is why all of the Africans I met while overseas had such a strong sense for family. Even if they held high profile positions such as a Minister within the government, they would never allow modern times to influence their traditional way of life.

"A Soldier's Story"

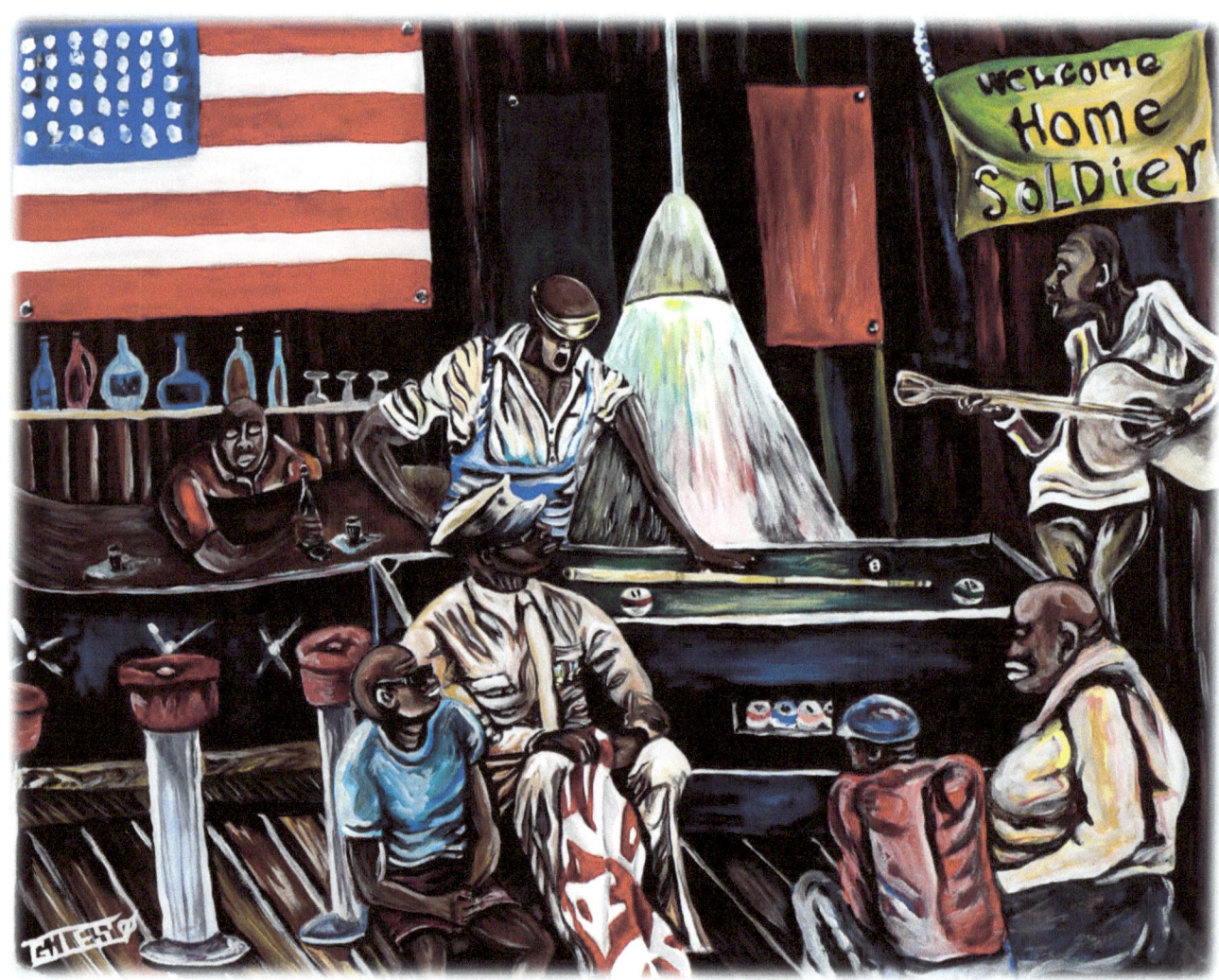

A Soldier's Story

I sit here with my brotha' and friends reflecting on my life in the military,

Attempting to compare it to those who served before me but coming short to the contrary.

I can only imagine because I wasn't there, but will try to put into words the true story of the soldiers who were not often treated fair.

Let me start you off with stories of soldiers from long ago,

A fierce fighter, who the Indians feared, said they were as dark as coal.

From the 24/25 infantry regiment, their hair wooly and out of the west,

Brave, strong, no enemy wanted to face them the "Buffalo Soldier", the Army's best!

Imagine these are runaway slaves dragged from Africa in fear,

Still loyal black soldiers wearing blue uniforms formed South Carolina's first volunteers.

Fifty thousand, the total black population during the Revolutionary War,

Despite this fact 3,000 gallant soldiers served at Bunker Hill, Yorktown, and many more.

4th, 5th, 6th and 7th Calvary African-American brothers continue to defend,

Although southern and northern racists choked on the idea of a uniform being worn by these men.

Battleship USS West Virginia in 1941 had a brother; a second class Mess Attendant who manned the guns,

Dorie Miller looked around for more gunners. He saw none, so he continued the fight against the invaders from the land of the "Rising Sun".

Blacks over the years showed their patriotism; so the thought of fighting in WWII was a cinch,

Even so, white racism was still prevalent. While in Fort Benning, Georgia Private Felix Hall, a black soldier was lynched.

WWII, the Tuskegee Airmen escorted bombers over the coast of North Africa skies; all successful missions,

Finally through force, a white five-star General "Hap" Arnold had to give them their recognition.

"We" have served in many battles in this country; however, it wasn't until 1964 the Civil Rights Act was signed,

Who would have guessed just over 50 years later that General Colin Powell would be the first African American to become head of the Joint Chiefs of Staff. It's about time!

Despite their courage, over 50 years no Black soldier won the "Medal of Honor" of heroism and this had to be fixed,

So, President Bill Clinton signed the Defense Authorization Act in nineteen hundred ninety-six.

Yes, we will continue to defend this great country toward God's own Glory,

Whether the Gulf War, Iraq, or Afghanistan, America will serve. It's been our legacy...it's our story!

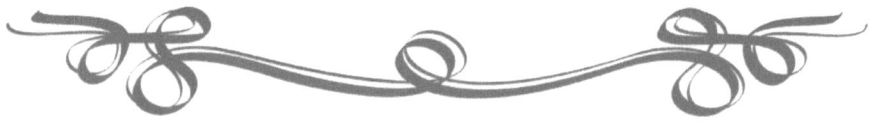

I actually did this picture when I was in high school. You can see the difference when you see my style of today. It's an acyclic painting with lots of color and the people are a little elongated. I was influenced by the artist, Ernie Barnes, who did the paintings that appeared on the television show, 'Good Times'. His work was always very colorful and expressive.

The pool hall is a common gathering place to meet up with friends, catch up on old times and of course, to have a scotch or two. This scene has a soldier reflecting on all the struggles military men and women have endured for this great country. He brings a little history to the group by relaying the efforts of the generation of soldiers who laid down their lives for this great country.

www.ingramcontent.com/pod-product-compliance
Lightning Source LLC
Chambersburg PA
CBHW050748180526
45159CB00003B/1384